MUSICAL INSTRUMENTS OF THE WORLD

Sound Effects

Barrie Carson Turner

Illustrated by John See

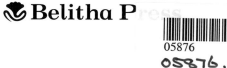

❧ Belitha Press

First published in the UK in 2000 by
 Belitha Press Limited
London House, Great Eastern Wharf,
Parkgate Road, London SW11 4NQ

Editor: Russell McLean
Designer: Zoe Quayle
Picture researcher: Juliet Duff
Educational consultant: Celia Pardaens
Consultant (bullroarer): Dr Hélène La Rue, Pitt Rivers Museum, Oxford

ISBN 1 84138 116 0

Printed in Singapore

British Library Cataloguing in Publication Data
for this book is available from the British Library.

10 9 8 7 6 5 4 3 2 1

Picture acknowledgements:
The Lebrecht Collection: 9; 21t, 21b Graham Salter; 10, 11,
14, 15, 19, 22, 24, 27, 29 Chris Stock. Performing Arts Library:
16 Clive Barda; 4-5, 18 Steve Gillett. Redferns: 23 Keith Hathaway;
6 Leon Morris; 12 Odile Noel; 7, 26 David Redfern.

Contents

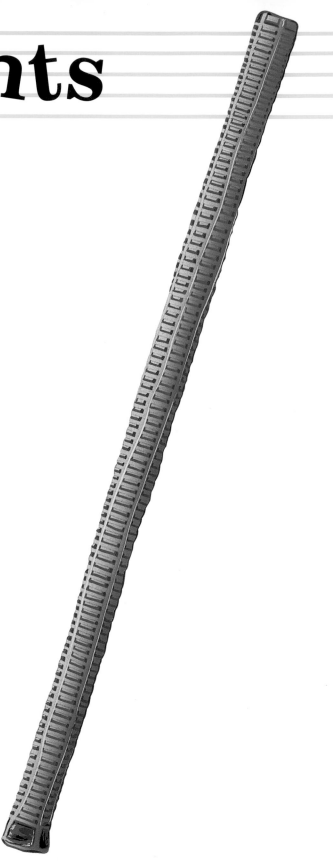

Musical

Musical instruments are played in every country of the world. There are many thousands of different instruments of all shapes and sizes. They are often divided into four groups: strings, brass, percussion and woodwind.

Percussion instruments are struck (hit), shaken or scraped to make their sound. Brass and woodwind instruments are blown to make their sound. String instruments sound when their strings vibrate.

instruments

This book is about instruments that can be used
to make sound effects. Sound effects often copy
a natural sound, such as the rumble of thunder,
or a galloping horse. They are used in the theatre,
on radio, and in film and television soundtracks.
Composers use them to create a special mood
in their music. Many of the sound effects in this
book are made by percussion instruments.

We have chosen 20 sound effects
instruments for this book. There is
a picture of each instrument and a
photograph of a performer playing
it. On pages 30 and 31 you
will find a list of useful words
to help you understand
more about music.

Cowbells

Traditional cowbells were hung around the necks of cattle. Inside each bell is a long metal clapper. The cowbell sounds when the clapper hits the sides of the instrument. In an orchestra, cowbells do not have clappers. They are struck with drum sticks to make them sound. The composer Gustav Mahler used cowbells in his Sixth Symphony to suggest the sounds of cattle in the Austrian countryside.

large bell sounds low notes

orchestral cowbells

small bell sounds high notes

In a band, cowbells are often fixed to a stand above tom-tom drums.

stand

6

Washboard

metal
sheet

ridges

metal
thimbles

The washboard is a wooden or metal board with ridges. Some washboards have a stand. Others are worn over the shoulders like a bib. Players scrape the washboard with a short metal bar, or with thimbles that are worn on the fingers.

The washboard is played in blues and jazz bands. It often marks the rhythm of the music.

Animal horns

Hundreds of years ago animal horns were blown by hunters. They were used to give signals – to call people together, for example. The animal horn illustrated here is a shofar. The instrument is made from the horn of a ram. Players blow into a mouthpiece at the thin end. The shofar can only make two notes. One note is high, the other is low.

ram's horn

This shofar player is wearing traditional Jewish robes.

The shofar is mentioned in the Bible. The instrument is still used to celebrate the Jewish New Year. Animal horns are played in several well-known pieces of music. The composer Richard Wagner used a cow's horn in some of his operas.

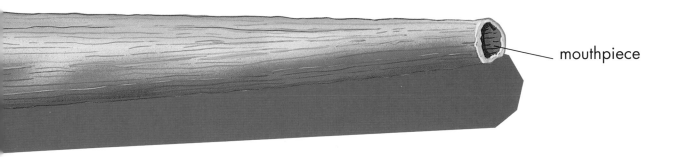

mouthpiece

Coconut shells

smooth and
hollow inside

hairy outside

Coconut shells are ancient instruments. They date back to prehistoric times. The shell of a coconut is split exactly in half. Then the white flesh inside is removed. Coconut shells are used to make the sound of horses' hoofs.

Coconut shells make a
crisp click when they
are tapped together.

10

Thunder sheet

The thunder sheet is made of thin steel. It hangs on a stand, and makes a deep rumbling sound. Large thunder sheets may be up to three metres high. The German composer Richard Strauss used this instrument in his *Alpine Symphony*.

stand

steel sheet

The thunder sheet is shaken by hand or struck with a soft beater to make it sound.

Handbells

Bells are very old instruments. Some bells are as large as a person, but handbells are small enough to be held in the hand. Players shake them to make several sounds, or gently flick them upwards to produce only one note.

A handbell group is called a team or a choir. Each musician usually plays two bells.

large bell sounds low notes

clapper

12

leather
handle

Inside each bell is a
metal clapper. When
the bell is swung, the
clapper hits the side
of the instrument and
the bell sounds. The bells
usually come in several
different sizes. Each
handbell sounds a
different note.

Handbells were traditionally
used as practice instruments
by church bell ringers.
Nowadays they are
played in concerts.

small bell
sounds
high notes

Anvil

The anvil makes a heavy clinking sound which is loud enough to be heard above a full orchestra. Sometimes a real blacksmith's anvil is played. Otherwise the orchestra uses a piece of thick steel called an anvil plate. You can hear anvils in the opera *Il Trovatore*, by the composer Giuseppe Verdi.

hammer

Musicians use hammers to play a traditional blacksmith's anvil.

thick, heavy steel

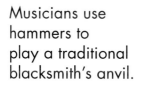

Flexatone

The flexatone has a handle, a thin metal sheet and two round wooden strikers. Each striker is fixed to a springy wire. When the instrument is shaken, the strikers hit the metal sheet, one after the other. This makes an unusual whining sound.

wooden striker

metal sheet

springy wire

Pressing on the metal sheet of the flexatone makes the notes higher or lower.

handle

15

Unusual sounds

Composers sometimes include unusual sounds in their music to create a special mood. In 1962, the composer György Ligeti wrote a piece of music for 100 metronomes called *Poème Symphonique*. A metronome has a metal arm that swings from side to side. It makes a steady clicking sound which is used to mark the beat of the music.

metal arm

movable weight

metronome

A typewriter and a row of bottles are some of the unusual instruments waiting to be played at this performance.

16

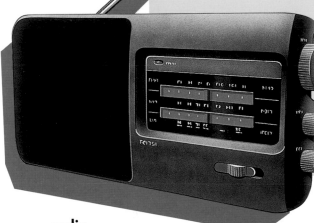

pipe

nightingale

metal bowl

air escape
hole

The Pines of Rome is a piece
of music by Ottorino Respighi.
It features a recording of a
nightingale singing. This sound can
also be made by a type of whistle called
a nightingale. The player blows air into
a pipe fixed to a bowl. The bowl is half
filled with water. The air makes a warbling
sound as it bubbles through the water.

The American composer
John Cage wrote a piece
of music for 12 radios.
It is called *Imaginary
Landscape Number 4.*

radio

Odaiko

The odaiko is a large drum from Japan. The instrument is shaped like a barrel. It has two heads, or skins, but usually only one head is played. The odaiko is used in Japanese theatre. The drum is often hidden at the side of the stage. Special drum strokes make the sound of the wind and the rain.

barrel-shaped body

iron ring for lifting

head

nails

wooden stand

The odaiko is so big that it has to be struck with large beaters to make a powerful sound.

Wind machine

This instrument makes a sound like the wind. Long, narrow boards of wood are built into the frame of a barrel. The outside of the barrel is covered with a sheet made of canvas or silk. As the handle is turned, the barrel spins round. The wooden boards brush against the sheet. This makes a rushing sound.

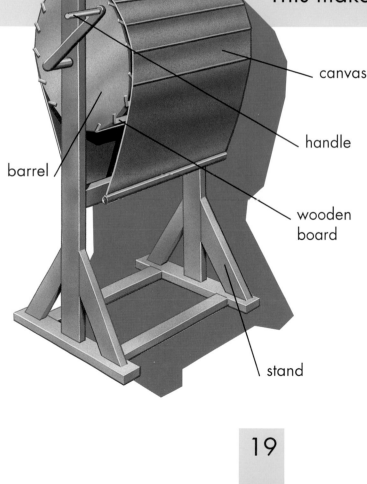

canvas

handle

barrel

wooden board

stand

The sound of the wind machine is made louder by turning the handle faster.

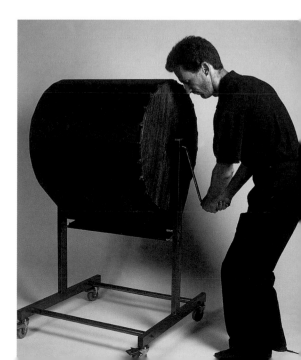

Bullroarer

hole

carved wood

Bullroarers are carved from a flat piece of wood, shell, bone or horn. There is a hole at one end. A long string is threaded through the hole. The performer holds the end of the string and whirls the instrument around their head. This makes a whirring sound. Small bullroarers make a high sound. Large instruments make a low sound. Other names for the bullroarer are thunder stick or whizzer.

20

Bullroarers have been used by tribes in Australia, North America and Africa since ancient times. In some places, people believed the instrument had magical powers, and that its sound was the voice of a spirit or an ancestor.

Bullroarers are often beautifully decorated. This large bullroarer will make a low sound.

As the bullroarer is swung faster, its sound becomes higher.

string

holding end

Cog rattle

The cog rattle is sometimes called a ratchet. Inside the frame are thin strips of wood. They are called tongues. A handle is attached to a wooden cog. When the handle is turned, the tongues of wood scrape against the cog. The cog rattle was used by Beethoven in his *Battle Symphony* to make the sound of rifle fire.

handle

frame hides wooden tongues

cog

A cog rattle makes a loud clacking sound when the handle is turned.

22

Whip

The whip is made from two long pieces of wood. They are joined together at one end by a hinge. The player holds the instrument with both hands. When the two pieces of wood are snapped together, they make a sound like the cracking of a whip. The instrument was first used in Austria, where it made the sound of a horse whip in a dance called the polka.

wooden board

hinge

handle

This large whip will make a very loud sound.

Sirens

The siren is often used to give signals – to warn against danger, for example. It makes a very powerful sound that can travel long distances. Sirens sound when air is forced through them. Air is blown into a mouth siren. An electric siren has air pumped through it by a fan.

mouthpiece

mouth siren

discs inside metal body

The mouth siren makes a high wailing sound. It is often used in comedy shows.

24

discs inside
metal body

electric
siren

electric cable

There are metal
discs inside both types of siren. Each disc
has holes in it. When air is forced through the siren,
the discs spin round. This makes a humming sound.
As the discs turn faster, the humming turns into a
rising, wailing sound. When the air stops blowing,
the wail falls slowly back to silence.

Rainstick

People in ancient times believed that playing the rainstick helped to bring rain for crops. The instrument is made by hollowing out a tree branch or a bamboo cane. This is filled with dried seeds or small stones. When the rainstick is held at a gentle angle, the seeds trickle to the bottom. This makes a sound like rain.

dried seeds or small stones (inside)

wooden or bamboo stick

Another name for the rainstick is rattling stick.

Chains

C hains have been used by several composers to add an unusual sound effect to their music. Chains are usually made of iron. They are moved up and down slowly to make a heavy clanking sound. The lower end of the instrument rests on the floor or on a metal sheet.

heavy iron chains

Chains are held in both hands. Heavy chains make the best sound.

Jingles

Jingles are tiny round bells. Inside each bell is a hard pellet made of metal or clay. The bells are fixed to a stick, a frame or a leather strap. Jingles are shaken to make a high tinkling sound. They have been played since ancient times, when they were sewn on to clothes and the bridles of horses. People believed that the jingles frightened away evil spirits.

jingle

pellet inside jingle

wooden handle

28

Jingles are also called sleigh bells, because they were fixed to horse-drawn sleighs. Today they are often played in Christmas music. The words of the song *Jingle Bells* describe a sleigh ride.

plastic frame

When jingles are shaken, the pellets rattle inside the bells, making a shimmering sound.

Words to

anvil A traditional blacksmith's anvil is a heavy block of iron or steel. Blacksmiths hammer hot pieces of metal into different shapes on an anvil.

bamboo A kind of tall grass with a hard, hollow stem.

beat The steady pulse of the music.

beaters Sticks of wood or wire used to strike some instruments. The ends may be made of felt or rubber.

blues A type of folk music that began in America around 100 years ago.

chords Groups of notes played together.

clapper A small piece of metal inside a bell. The clapper strikes the sides of the bell to make it sound.

composer Someone who writes pieces of music. See page 31 for more information on the composers in this book.

head The part of a drum that is struck. It is also called the skin.

jazz A kind of pop music. Jazz musicians often make up the music at the same time as they play it.

melody A tune.

mouthpiece The part of a wind instrument that is held in the mouth. Musicians blow into the mouthpiece.

opera A musical play in which actors sing their parts.

orchestra A large group of musicians playing together.

pellet A tiny ball made of wood, metal or another hard material.

remember

pitch How high or low a sound is.

polka A fast dance that appeared in Europe in about 1830.

rhythm A rhythm is made by the beat of the music, and by how long and short the notes are.

scraper Any instrument that is scraped to make it sound.

soundtrack The music which accompanies a film or a television programme.

strike To play an instrument by hitting it.

thimble A small metal cap which is worn on a finger.

tongue A thin strip of wood.

vibrate To shake very quickly from side to side.

Composers in this book

Ludwig van Beethoven (German, 1770–1827) wrote symphonies, piano sonatas and string quartets.

Richard Wagner (German, 1813–1883) is famous for his operas, which are based on ancient myths and legends.

Giuseppe Verdi (Italian, 1813–1901) wrote some of Italy's greatest operas.

Gustav Mahler (Austrian, 1860–1911) was a great symphony composer and conductor.

Richard Strauss (German, 1864–1949) was a conductor and composer. He wrote orchestral music and operas.

Ottorino Respighi (Italian, 1879–1936) wrote operas and colourful orchestral music.

John Cage (American, 1912–1992) was a musical experimenter who wrote unusual and original music.

György Ligeti (Hungarian, born 1923) has written electronic music, as well as instrumental and vocal works.

Index